First published in 2008 by Wayland
Text copyright © Pat Thomas 2008
Illustrations copyright © Lesley Harker 2008

Wayland
338, Euston Road,
London NW1 3BH

Wayland Australia
Hachette Children's Books
Level 17/207 Kent Street
Sydney, NSW 2000

Concept design: Kate Buxton
Series design: Jean Scott Moncrieff

British Library Cataloguing in Publication Data
Thomas, Pat, 1959–
Why is it so hard to breathe? : a first look at asthma
1. Asthmatics – Juvenile literature 2. Asthma – Juvenile literature
I. Title II. Lesley, Harker
616.2'38

ISBN-13: 9780750252362

Printed in China

Wayland is a division of Hachette Children's Books,
an Hachette Livre UK company.

Why is it so Hard to Breathe?

A FIRST LOOK AT ASTHMA

PAT THOMAS
ILLUSTRATED BY LESLEY HARKER

WAYLAND

Would you like to know something amazing? You breathe air in and out of your lungs thousands of times a day.

6

Most of the time breathing is so easy that we never have to think about it. But for some people breathing can sometimes be really hard. These people have asthma.

7

When a really bad asthma attack comes it can be frightening.

You may find yourself coughing or wheezing and gasping for air.

It may feel as if a giant is sitting on your chest stopping you from getting any air in.

What about you?

What happens when you have an asthma attack?
What does it feel like to you when you can't breathe?

Asthma is an illness that makes it hard to get
enough air into your lungs.

You can get it when you are an adult, but most people are either born with it or get it when they are very young.

Asthma is not like a cold – you can't catch it from someone.

And you can't always tell just by looking whether another person has asthma. Most of the time people with asthma breathe just like everyone else.

When you first find out you have asthma
you may feel worried and you may have
a lot of questions.

Your parents and your doctor will be able to help you understand more about what causes your asthma and what you can do.

Your doctor might give you a test. He or she may ask you to blow one big puff into a special tube.

This tube measures how much air you can blow out all at once. People with asthma blow out less air than other people.

If your doctor thinks you have asthma, he
or she may also give you some other tests to
see if you have any allergies that might
cause your asthma.

Although asthma can't be cured, there are lots of ways to control it. Your doctor might give you medicine in something called an inhaler.

With an inhaler you breathe medicine straight into your lungs.

Some inhalers are used in the morning to
prevent attacks during the day.

Some you can carry with you to make
it easier to breathe if you feel wheezy
during the day.

Lots of things can make asthma worse
including allergies to things in the air.

dust

mould

smoke

pet's fur

feathers

traffic fumes

pollen

Cold weather and exercising without first
warming up your muscles can also make it worse.

Having a cold or being scared or unhappy
can also make your asthma worse.

What about you?

Do you know the things that make your asthma worse?
Are you good at avoiding them?

As you get older you will learn to keep away from the things that make your asthma worse.

You'll also learn to keep your inhaler with you and know when an attack is coming.

The people who care about you - your parents, teachers and friends - will also need to learn about these things to help you stay healthy.

Asthma can be a pain.
Sometimes it might feel as if
you can't do the fun things
everyone else does.

But people with asthma can do almost anything.

In fact, lots of famous sports people, singers
and people you see on TV have asthma.

They've learned that as long as they take a bit of extra care, having asthma doesn't mean they have to miss out on anything fun. And pretty soon you will find that out for yourself too!

HOW TO USE THIS BOOK

Whenever you talk to your child about health matters it's best to be honest, open and positive. Tell your child that asthma can't always be cured (only about half of children who have asthma 'grow out of it') but that medicine can help control the symptoms. Talk about the equipment your child may encounter such as peak flow monitors, nebulizers and different types of inhalers.

Be patient. Children in the four to seven age group will not fully understand their condition and cannot be expected to be in complete control of their environments in order to avoid all asthma triggers. At this age they will understand that they have lungs that help them breathe, that asthma makes breathing difficult and that certain things make asthma worse. But they may still expose themselves to triggers and risks if they are part of a group or if it looks like fun. Likewise they can understand and assist with medicines, but it is up to parents and other carers to provide help and supervision.

As early as you can, make sure your child learns to recognize the things that trigger an asthma attack and reinforce the need to avoid these things. With a slightly older child, it is worth exploring alternative breathing techniques such as those used in yoga or the Buteyko method. These can help your child breathe more fully and can help calm breathing when he or she feels an attack coming on.

Different children react to asthma differently. It's important to tailor your approach to your child and provide the right level of reassurance and empathy. As often as possible, help your child understand that while asthma can't be ignored, it doesn't mean that he or she can't live a normal life. You may wish to find out about famous people who have asthma and discuss these with your child to show them that what asthmatics do and achieve in life isn't limited by their disease. While your child is coming to terms with asthma, encourage descriptive, feeling words to describe symptoms.

Communication with carers and teachers is the key. If your child has asthma you will need to work with other adults who may care for him or her so that everyone knows what triggers to avoid and what to do if the child has an attack. Make sure you know of any activities that might impact your child's asthma. If you wish your child's health problems to remain confidential at school this should be respected.

In school, learning about asthma can be covered through health education (how the lungs work and what allergies are, for instance) and also through science (e.g. understanding environmental triggers such as pollen). Many pupils may have experience of asthma: they may have it themselves, or have a family member with asthma, or a friend may have the condition.

An interesting way to get children who don't have asthma to understand what it feels like is to stage a simple exercise. Have the children run in place for one minute. They should be breathing hard and fast when they finish. When they stop, tell them to block their noses, put a straw in their mouths and close their lips around it, and then try to breathe through the straw (they should only do this for a few seconds). This will give them an indication of how hard it can be to get air into the lungs when the airways have closed up.

BOOKS TO READ

When It's Hard to Breathe
Judith Condon (Franklin Watts, 1998)

Asthma
Sarah Lennard Brown (Wayland, 2002)

It's Not Catching...Asthma
Angela Royston (Heinemann First Literature, 2004)

All About Asthma
William Ostrow, Vivian Ostrow, Blanche Sims
(Concept Books, 1989)

Living With Asthma
Peta Bee (Wayland, 2005)

RESOURCES FOR ADULTS

Asthma UK
Summit House
70 Wilson Street
London
EC2A 2DB
Tel: 020 7786 4900
Helpline: 08457 010203
www.asthma.org.uk

Allergy UK
3 White Oak Square
London Road
Swanley
Kent
BR8 7AG
Helpline: 01322 619898
www.allergyuk.org

British Society for Allergy, Environmental and Nutritional Medicine
PO Box 7
Knighton
Powys
LD & 2WF
Tel: 01547 550380
www.jnem.demon.co.uk

British Lung Foundation
73-75 Goswell Road
London EC1V 7ER
Helpline: 08458 50 50 20
www.lunguk.org

Buteyko Breathing Association
15 Stanley Place
Chipping Ongar
Essex
CM5 9SU
Tel: 01277 366906
www.buteykobreathing.org